THE OCEAN ABOVE

2016 POETRY COLLECTION

by Eric Nixon

Cover image: "NGC 7635: The Bubble Nebula" by NASA, ESA, and the Hubble Heritage Team (STScI / AURA).

Cover design by Eric Nixon.

ISBN-13: 978-0998436210
ISBN-10: 0998436216
BISAC: Poetry / American / General

Published by Double Yolk Press in Portland, Oregon.
EricNixonAuthor@gmail.com
EricNixon.net

DEDICATION

For you.

AUTHOR'S FOREWARD

If history were set up like some kind of weird series of museums, 2016 would probably suffer from a lack of attendance since it was such a shitty year for most people that they would not want to pay money to go back and re-visit it.

That's probably a poor lead-in paragraph to introduce you to my new poetry collection, written in and inspired by the year 2016.

Blerg.

2016 was terrible, yes. It was also the year I wrote the fewest number of poems since I started publishing an annual poetry collection. In this case, one has nothing to do with the other. The bulk of my free time this past year was spent working on my science fiction novel, *2492: Attack Of The Ancient Cyborg.*

Novels are huge, unwieldy things that take an immense amount of time to create and edit into something nicely presentable to the public. This was certainly true for *2492* as it took me 30 years to create from initial concept to completion. At some point I just wanted to finish it and get it out there, so I dove into it, editing the book like crazy until it was finally done. I'm very happy with the result, but it did take me away from my poetic routine resulting in a much smaller poetry collection this year compared to my previous collections.

Which is probably a good thing since this was 2016 we're talking about.

Enjoy!

Eric
January 14, 2017

TABLE OF CONTENTS

April – 2 poems
Waiting For Things
Who Wins

May – 4 poems
Coffee Ninja
Today Is What It Means To Be Alive
Within The Radius
Mentos Dropped

June – 1 poem
Helmet In The Street

July – 7 poems
Expressing Emotions With Firearms
The Ultimate Chicken And Egg
Of Someone Leaving A Job
A Quiet Time Much Too Long
Downpouring
The Joyous Sheen
The Answer

August – 5 poems
Out Of The Hatred Closet
Overlush
In The Neon Playground
Avoidance On The Strip
Leg Of A Rainbow

September – 2 poems
Sharing The Sunset
The Ocean Above

October – 10 poems
The Speed Of Things
Gorge Gone
Not What It Used To Be
I Didn't Need That Calculator After All
Everything Wrong With America
Walkman Nights
Which Is It?
A Cutter In Fronter
Early Voting
We're Not Participating This Year

November – 5 poems
What Should Have Been
All Of A Sudden, Everything Changed
Privilege Pass
Escape The Leftovers
Such Trivial Things

December – 6 poems
Targeted The Woman
My Pile Of Accomplishment
Just Barely, Just Now
Thanks For Finally Asking
Everyone Out Of The Pool
Some Years

2016 total: 70

JANUARY

Playing Pretendsy

Grown men playing pretendsy with their
Freshly-ironed military-looking fatigues
Holding something insignificant hostage
Demanding attention like a little kid tantrum
If it weren't for their very real weapons
No one would take the cowards seriously
Instead, their tactics ensure that remains the case
As America keeps the dildo parade
Raining steadily down upon them
Along with anything and everything
That could possibly make a mockery
Of the sad-sorry, tough-talking "men"
Who are afraid that the country they once knew
Is changing in ways they can't handle
And have no other way to express it
But by lashing out in a childish manner

January 17, 2016
Portland, Oregon

I'm torn about those jackhole militia dudes who took over that bird
sanctuary in Oregon. A part of me that I'm uncomfortable
acknowledging wants a bomb dropped on that place and for it to be
over and done with. No more soapbox for them. Done. Done.
Done. That other part of me is impressed with the psychological
aspect of the government's treatment of them. The longer this
continues, the less America will tolerate it. Plus, everyone sending
them things like bags of Gummy Bear-like dicks, dildos, and lube
is super funny and making a mockery of them and their cause. I'm
sure that's gotta be wearing them down.

What bothers me more is the double standard of the situation;
unarmed black man doing something wrong equals death, Judge
Dredd-style. A group of militarized white men commit a terroristic
act and threaten to kill police equals free reign to do whatever they
please.

January

I Have A Problem With Time's Limitations

Previous to this
I must have lived
In some sort of place
Where all time existed
Simultaneously; everything at once
Where you could pick and choose
The things you paid attention to
When you wanted them
That cool band coming to town?
Why not save seeing them
Until you've got the chance
Even if it's years later.
Hesitant to act on something
Until you have more information?
Now you can jump in feet-first
Because you know everything.
I'm certain this is what I'm used to
Because for my entire life
I've missed events comfortably
With the mindset that I can always
Just go back and enjoy it at a later date
And it's taken me nearly forty-two years
To discover that no, I can't do that here
I have a problem with time's limitations
Which is a damn shame
Because I really liked living
With that comfort
That seems unavailable
Here on Earth

> January 17, 2016
> Portland, Oregon

Seriously. My entire life I've lived like this. A cool band is coming
to town and I don't end up seeing them. Months later I'll think,
"Ok, I'm ready to see them now," and I can't. But the thing is it

seems so completely normal to me that I *should* be able to do whatever I want *whenever* I want.

The Truth

The truth is
None of us
Really know
Anything
Beyond
What we see
And experience
So be sure to
See and experience
Everything possible
That way you'll
Know it all

> January 17, 2016
> Portland, Oregon

Ha!

This Really Isn't Anything

This really isn't anything
Other than me occupying
Myself for a few minutes
My mind listening to music
My fingers on the keyboard
Typing and writing nothing
While waiting for the guest
Occupying my bathroom
To finish so I can get in there

January 16, 2016
Portland, Oregon

The sister of one of our friends from Massachusetts is in Portland checking out colleges. I'm just…never mind, she's out.

Mossening

A cement block wall
Situated in a city
Known for its rain
Located in a place
Where it gets no sun
Becomes naturally overgrown
With a thick carpet
Of the mossening
Covering every last bit
Brightening the color
With a natural hue
And, in turn
Beautifying the space

> January 18, 2016
> Portland, Oregon

Walking through my neighborhood tonight, I saw a wall that was
coated very thickly in moss and it looked really neat.

Your Cat Was Cute Today On Instagram

Things people now say
When they meet face to face,
Don't really know each other,
And want to compliment them
But can't think of anything else:
"Your cat was cute today on Instagram"

> January 18, 2016
> Portland, Oregon

Half A God

Hanging your hat upon
And letting who you are
Be solely defined
By half an Amendment
Makes about as much sense
As praying to half a god
And making that the thing
You're forever known for
Either way, you're crazy

January 18, 2016
Portland, Oregon

They always seem to conveniently forget the other half.

Spaghetti Back

Spaghetti back:
Enticing clothing
Or a messy meal
Your choice:
One
The other
Or both at once

> January 18, 2016
> Portland, Oregon

Too silly.

A Dour-Gray Squelching Tint

There is nothing that invokes
More emotions than the thought
Of a high-school reunion
Several hours of being social
With those who have known you
Intimately from pre-school, onward
Through the most awkward portion
Of our lives; those damnable years
We'd most like to erase and forget
All of the fears, the embarrassments,
The terrible knowledge they know
About each and every other person
Now decades removed from reality
But brought back piercingly into these moments
Along with a full and open bar
To properly liquefy and enhance
The flow of remembrances
And the details of the fuzziest memories
Combined with not having aged so well
Adds an extra stressor to the situation
Along with knowing those super-achievers
Who have accomplished mind-boggling feats
Will be there, front and center, ready to share
And while I've had a pretty great life
I still feel like I don't measure up
And I know that's completely wrong to think
But I'm human, after all
And this is what we all think
When we're alone with our inward thoughts
And the insecurities begin to creep in
And discolor the memories
Like some never-used Instagram filter
That overly darkens everything
With a dour-gray squelching tint
That once you saw for the first time
You'd vow to never want to see again

January 18, 2016
Portland, Oregon

Yikes! I've got like a year and a half until my 25th reunion (if we even have one), and I'm already stressing about it and I don't know why. I missed my 20th reunion, but I think I would go to my next one, and I'd probably have a great time. Most of my classmates seem to have gotten really cool (according to social media, which doesn't at all, in any way, paint people in overly perfect lighting).

Making The Medium

While they're busying themselves
Throwing their hat collections
One-by-one, into every ring
Chasing the kudos, the prizes,
The recognition that comes with
Marketers making the medium
About them, their resumes,
And their well-polished mirrors.
I'm steering clear of the scene
Leaving this me, Me, ME town,
Eschewing the roads and
Finding myself by myself
Writing about what the Universe
Has put within reach of my senses
And making the medium
About what it really is:
A form of communication
To convey, to explain, to show
My experience with you
And no one else

        January 19, 2016
        Portland, Oregon

Forefront

Can you question
The mind's eye
When it can
Clearly see
All things
Real or imagined
Right there
Forefront
In your thoughts
From vivid memories
To casual thoughts
To the fictional neverhappened
And everything in-between
It's all there
Easily imagined
Like TV for your mind
That only you,
And governments of the future,
Can watch

> January 23, 2016
> Portland, Oregon

To me, "neverhappened" is most definitely a real word. This is why I'm a terrible Scrabble player.

When Did We Get So Wimpy About Snow

As a child growing up in the Berkshires
In the hills of Western Massachusetts
It seemed like snowfalls and snow squalls
Of two to three feet were routine and normal
And considered normal business in winter
When did we get so wimpy about snow?
Where a foot or two of snow is now akin
To crippling action, to total destruction
To something that no one can possibly handle
As disaster areas are declared and people die
This never used to happen when I was a kid
We got snowed in, we dug out, and that was it
And there was nothing more to say about the matter

January 23, 2016
Portland, Oregon

I think climate change has made everyone unreasonably soft when it comes to normal winter conditions.

Pretty Chicken #2

In the window of a store
Sat a formerly live
But now stuffed chicken.
Around it's neck
Hung a sign saying,
"Pretty chicken # 2."
The words were true
It was certainly pretty
But I looked and wondered
Where its friend was
Had it been sold?
Was "Pretty chicken # 1"
Even more alluring?
We may never know.

January 23, 2016
Portland, Oregon

This one has been in my Line Ideas document when Kari and I stayed at the Union Street Guest House in Hudson, New York on our retreat to plan for the coming year of 2013. We stopped by a neat store that had all manner of weird and neat objects, including "Pretty Chicken #2." I didn't end up changing anything about my poetic notes and am publishing it as I had originally wrote it back then. Sometimes it just takes some time to realize something was ready all along.

Patience, And August Comes

Patience, and August comes
Was a name of a post
On a friend's website
Written in the drowning deep heat
Of July's all-enveloping oppression
Which struck a chord in me
As I bided my time waiting
For the 100-degree days to pass
And the cooler, more refreshing months
Like September and everything thereafter
To finally arrive and save us all
From the summer months
And the side-effects
No one really wanted

January 23, 2016
Portland, Oregon

Last summer was brutal in how terribly hot it was. During that time, Alana Chernila did a blog post on her site called, "Patience, And August Comes." I really liked that phrase a lot because I was also biding my time, not for August, but for September and cooler months.

Another Lost Weekend

Something as innocuous as a dog
Cuddling up to you on the couch
Can delay the day and hand you
Yet another lost weekend
In the form of an unexpected nap
Blinking through the hours
And making the free minutes
Just that much more valuable

                    January 30, 2016
                    Portland, Oregon

Damnit, Baxter!

A Trail

I see myself as a person,
Walking through the woods of time
Leaving a trail of poems in my wake
Inviting others to join my on my journey
Years after the fact
And hope they see
And enjoy the time
We spend together
With me being their personal tour guide
To the landscape and scenery
The Universe has provided me

January 30, 2016
Portland, Oregon

I was just looking at the stack of seven books I've written on my desk beside me. In the past year, I've come to realize that these poems are a sort of a diary, in a way. Just now, I thought that people don't get to read what I've written until years after the fact, and these poems are like a trail of breadcrumbs left in the woods…either for me to find my way back home, or for the readers to follow me on my journey through life.

When The Big Thoughts Come

When the big thoughts come
Everything else gets pushed
Aside
Away
The daily humanity becomes
A distraction
Unimportant
Compared to the hugeness
Of the deepest delvings
The ones that threaten
To consume
To remove
Me from everything I know
And I'm secretly ok with that
Because getting lost
In the endless thoughts
That wholly comprise
The entirety of creation
From the fractions of
The tiniest nano particles
To giant clusters of galaxies
And the energy that
Binds it all together
Binds us all together
Are the ones worth thinking
And maybe getting lost there
Over and over, enough times,
Will someday,
Help us find our way

January 31, 2016
Portland, Oregon

January

FEBRUARY

Purposely Ignoring The Ringing

Nature is the keeper of the switch
Which, once flicked, changes the seasons
From cold and snowy to warm and pretty
And eventually flips back once again
But something's been wrong in the recent past
Where, late in the year, the switch has been sticking
In the "Warm" position for too long
Or, in the Winter, it has a tendency
To switch seasons all by itself
Worried, Nature tried calling a repairperson
But no one answered, and no one came
So Nature is doing it's best to manage
By adapting, calling, and waiting
Meanwhile things are getting topsy-turvy
All because the ones who can fix things
Are purposely ignoring the ringing

February 7, 2016
Portland, Oregon

Forgotten Leftovers

The four who chose to remain
Are nothing but forgotten leftovers
No news crews covering the story
Because there is no longer any story
And our attention has moved on;
Sure there may be a blip of news
When they are finally arrested or shot
Just wait a quarter-second later
And their story will be forgotten

February 7, 2016
Portland, Oregon

Silly militants.

Early February Sunny Sunday Day

Unseasonably warm, mid-sixties
Early February sunny Sunday day
Enticed out the entirety of the city
To bask, absorb, and soak up the sun
Like life-sized human sponges
After months of dreary gray rain
To feel a changed day like this
Was to be like a prisoner released
By the instant change in the season
That once held us inside our homes
And has now granted our freedom

February 7, 2016
Portland, Oregon

Holy wow, it was nice today.

The Joy Of The Push

Playful
Like a cat
Innocently knocking
Everything off a dresser
It knows only
The joy of the push
And the falling of the object
And the shattering it makes on the floor
Beyond that, it doesn't know or care
Only the moment
It lives so completely in

February 7, 2016
Portland, Oregon

One Day

I would like to think
That one day
Someday
Someone
Will read something I wrote
And enjoy it
And one day
This day, today,
I would like to thank
That someone
For reading something I wrote

February 7, 2016
Portland, Oregon

Thank you!

Ponies And Kittens

Tonight was the
BIG AMERICAN SPORT-BALL GAME
That had ponies on one side
Pitted against kittens
From what the news tells me
The ponies won
Which really isn't surprising
Since they have much longer legs
And aren't as easily distracted
Don't worry kittens
Not a lick of it truly matters
Because it's just a silly game

February 7, 2016
Portland, Oregon

Ten Cents

Overly chatty young guy cashier
Ringing me up on a rainy Saturday
I was hardly paying attention
To the ramblings he was saying
Something about *I Dream Of Jeanie*
And I barely even noticed
When the total was displayed:
$33.43
But I sure did pay attention
When he re-scanned an item
And made an adjustment
Of exactly ten cents
Bringing our grand total down to:
$33.33
He said in all the time he's cashiered
He's never seen a repeating number
Something he's always wanted
And he made it happen with us
So he said we were his favorite
Because we were the ones
Who made this happen for him
Like a divine alignment of order
In the sea of random numbers
He normally sees
In an average shift

February 13, 2016
Portland, Oregon

This happened today.

A Mountain Sliced

Driving home
Across the bridge
Across the border
I dared a look to my left
And after a triple-take
I finally made sense
Of the out-of-place scene
Developing on Mount Hood
A view that rarely changes
But today, a lenticular cloud
Had smoothed over
The sharp, tented point
And hugged the slope down
Until the half-way mark
Where it trailed straight out
Like a mountain sliced
Right through the middle
And the snowy interior
Sprayed like white blood
From the fatal wound
Carried with the motion
Of the unseen sword
Hefted by some sort of
Mountain-slaying giant
Revenging its grudge
Against the towering peak
Sending a message
To the now-fearful
And scared Mount Adams
Sandwiched between
The decapitated St. Helens
And the dying Mount Hood

February 16, 2016
Portland, Oregon

45

That was a weird cloud I saw today. I wish I could have gotten a photo of it. It really looked like Mount Hood had gotten sliced through the middle with a sword as the cloud ran down the slope and then straight out and away from the mountain for about two miles. I don't know where I was going there at the end of the poem but it sort of makes sense.

Look Out The Window

I look out the window
At the freedom beyond
And the heaviness holds me
Here, stuck in this place
Unable to move or do much
Or so I have been conditioned to think
Until the day I go outside
Breathe in the fresh, filling air
And find my feet lifting, floating
Up and off the ground
As the weighty responsibilities
Dissolve and dissipate
Lightening the load
Freeing my soul
Allowing me to expand
In ways previously unknown
All for the singularly fair price
Of temporary loneliness

February 28, 2016
Portland, Oregon

I was standing at my kitchen sink last night, looked out the window and saw one across-the-street neighbor staring out her window. At the house beside hers was another person not just staring out the window, but walking out the door and leaving the house. That got me thinking about the woman, with her family, who maybe feels stuck in her house; burdened with a hefty mortgage, no privacy, and a family who is always there. To me, she seemed like someone who would be yearning for freedom. The house next to hers is made up of a few roommates. Over there, they have that freedom to be able to leave whenever they want; they're young, have disposable income, no spouses, no kids, no mortgage, nothing holding them down. I took the two sides of that view and mushed them together to create this poem.

Extended By A Day

A year
Longer by
A day
What will be done?
What will you do
To make it special
Will you take advantage
Of this extra time?
Will you do great things
With the year
Extended by a day?
Or will it pass on by
Just like any other?

> February 29, 2016
> Portland, Oregon

February

The Ocean Above

MARCH

A Life Or Death Moment

A scheduled doctor visit for her
With a doctor who was unsure
And sent her to the hospital
To get something checked out
So we went, just to see what it was
The ultrasound guy did his thing
And immediately found the trouble
A very serious issue
And recommended she go
To the emergency room
To which she put her foot down
And said no, she wanted to go home
He left the room and gave us a minute
Which was when the déjà vu hit me
Like a fisted hammer intent on harm
Where I saw with perfect clarity
This room, this moment, we were in
The empty ultrasound tech's chair
The empty chair off to one side
The color of the walls
And every other possible detail
That I KNEW I had seen before
But what was worse
Was the future I also knew
Because within my déjà vu
I saw her continue to refuse
And then we left the hospital
And the next thing I knew
I was standing at home in a room
The newly hollow me filled
Overflowing with a deep sadness
On a day I knew to be a work day
But I also knew I was using
Bereavement days to be here
Where I struggled with the shock
Of her passing and fought to cope
With what to do with all of her stuff

And how to continue living my life
Alone
And as the déjà vu feeling faded
And I returned back to the present
There in the ultrasound room
With her, alive and now
I realized that this very second
Was a life or death moment
And that if we went one way
She would die within days
And if we went the other
She would be just fine
So I told her what I saw
Which changed her mind
And before we knew it
The ultrasound guy
Was wheelchairing her down the hall
And casually mentioning
He was stunned she was even alive

Thankfully she remained that way

> March 6, 2016
> Portland, Oregon

The discovery of a near-fatal blood clot (the biggest any of the doctors had ever seen) and the thankful wallop of déjà vu that saved Kari's life.

The Ocean Above

APRIL

Waiting For Things

Waiting for things
To click into place
Is driving me crazy
In this year of change
In the year I'm supposed
To break free of the things
Holding me back and down
And get going on my real life
To finally take charge and move
On with the half-used person I am
To make something real and concrete
That others will find useful in some way
Until then, I'm simply waiting to get going

April 7, 2016
Portland, Oregon

Or, more appropriately titled, "Shapes Of Things." I got stuck on
the shape that was developing as I wrote and focused just on that.

Who Wins

The gloves are off
The teeth are out
Niceties have been
Neatly dispensed with
And the hammer of truth
Is swinging strongly
In both directions
Aiming for a solid hit
Hoping for a quick kill
But no, instead it drags on
Until the bucket of lies
Gets thrown, dousing,
Burning, disfiguring,
Unfairly branding
First one, then the other
Because by this point
Who wins is of no matter
It's who can permanently scar
Their opponent the most

April 7, 2016
Portland, Oregon

I hate presidential election season. The president should serve one
eight-year term with no reelection possible, just to save us from the
scripted spectacle we have to endure every four years.

MAY

Coffee Ninja

I almost spilled coffee on me
But I was stealth, like ninja fast
And I got out of the way
With plenty of time to spare
And caught the splash
Back in my same cup
And drank it nonchalantly
Like it was no biggie
I'm such a good thing
I'm a coffee ninja

May 8, 2016
Portland, Oregon

Silly. Based on something my boss said a few weeks ago.

Today Is What It Means To Be Alive

Not yesterday, none of that past stuff
You've lived it once, never again
Don't waste time retracing your steps
Not tomorrow, full of promise and promises
With your head stuck in dreams
Which seem to always live
The same tomorrow away
Today is what it means to be alive
Not just today,
Which is made up of both past and future,
But right now
This moment here, this very second
The one you're perpetually stuck in
That's the very one where you need to be
In order to fully appreciate your life
In order to start doing something
To change the direction you're heading
In order to take action and get to accomplishing
All of those dreams you've been having
Right now, close this book
Get out of this chair
Stand up, and get going
Working on realizing everything
You've ever wanted
And making yourself proud
For taking that first step
In this very moment
Where you saw and knew
What it meant to be alive
And did something about it

May 8, 2016
Portland, Oregon

Sometimes I feel obligated to balance the silly poems with ones
that are almost too deep.

Within The Radius

Within the radius
Of something great
Always and all the time
But never lucky enough
To be the target
Or the subject
Of that greatness
Instead I get to witness
As friends of friends
Achieve the success
I've secretly longed for
With effortless ease
As if it were nothing
So I watch and I learn
And wonder what I'll do
And how I'll react
When that radius shrinks
Until it surrounds
Nothing but me

> May 8, 2016
> Portland, Oregon

Someday.

Mentos Dropped

Mentos dropped
In a full 2-liter bottle
And quickly capped
To contain the blast
That's trapped inside
The frothing twisting
Bulging and stretching
The twisted vessel
Wanting nothing more
Than to release
The tortuous pressure
Bringing it
To the breaking point
Completely dependent
On the one who started this
To lend a hand
And twist open the cap
Bringing the flood
Of pressurized foam
Wasted everywhere
Dependent on the one
Who is most likely
To refuse to help
As they watch
With fascinated glee
As the bottle
Is torn apart
By the pressures
Built up within

        May 8, 2016
        Portland, Oregon

That simple, fun, science experiment as told through the view of the soda bottle.

The Ocean Above

JUNE

Helmet In The Street

On a moped heading home
Like thousands of times before
Moment to moment
Nothing new, just like always
Routinely driving home
Thinking about–

Lights swing TOO CLOSE
Impact, crunch, airborne
Crushed and grated
On the pavement
Mundane to critical
Faster than a heartbeat
Bodily functions crashing
Things are incredibly wrong
But nothing can be done
Barely aware of voices
Apologies, yelling, murmurs
The close voice saying
Everything will be ok
Is a damn dirty liar
The quiet voices
Further away are more honest
With their wide-eyed assessment
Far-off sirens grow closer
And so does the darkness
As the two engage in a race
Painfully, agonizingly slow
And at this point,
Beyond endurance,
I don't care who wins
Or if I will get to see
Tomorrow's article about this
With the pausing photo
Of my helmet in the street
Surrounded by the debris
Caused by the other's

Careless moment

June 20, 2016
Portland, Oregon

Last week there was a crash a block away from our house. An
SUV was turning left and didn't see the moped driving straight in
the opposite direction. I got to the intersection just before the
ambulance and saw people tending to the injured guy. A minute
later help arrived and took him away. His helmet was left lying in
the street.

The Ocean Above

JULY

Expressing Emotions With Firearms

Little scared boys
Deep in and well past
Middle age but still living
In the Middle Ages
Latching onto a line
As the words to live
And kill others by
Fueled by macho movies
And an inflated sense
Of overconfidence
By the piece on their waist
Frightened of words
And regular societal discourse
They know nothing else other than
Expressing emotions with firearms
Because silencing all other voices
With a reflexive finger pull
Is so much easier than listening
Or thinking

        July 18, 2016
        Portland, Oregon

July

The Ultimate Chicken And Egg

"…the ultimate chicken and egg…"
Was the fragment of a line I overheard
From a guy on a phone across the street
Last night while I was walking the dogs
And I wished I could hear the other end
Of that instantly fascinating conversation
And it got me wondering about what
The Ultimate Chicken And Egg was:
Maybe a new breakfast at Denny's?
Or an animated movie from Japan?
The pinnacle of philosophical debate?
An aviary award from the county fair?
Whatever this quandary shaped up to be
It had my brain running overtime
And, I'll never know the answer
Unless I make it up and say,
"Yes, that's it. That's the answer
To The Ultimate Chicken And Egg."

July 18, 2016
Portland, Oregon

71

Of Someone Leaving A Job

You have to pity the stupidity
Of someone leaving a job
Without something else lined up
But
You have to admire the morality
Of someone leaving a job
Who no longer finds joy in it

July 30, 2016
Portland, Oregon

My boss gave his notice yesterday and called me to let me know personally. It's something that's stuck hard in the back of my mind as to what would drive someone to leave a comfortable regional job in his life-long career; to part so easily with a company he's worked with for nearly a decade. The trouble I'm having with it is I'm stuck between the, "What an idiot!" and "Damn, I really admire someone who puts his happiness first."

Good luck.

A Quiet Time Much Too Long

Windows down
Speeding down along the Interstate
Radio off
No sound but the engine humming and the wind blowing
Sunlight dissipating
Diffusing in the growing darkness
Hills blending
Into one another, punctuated by houses
Rural living
Wondering who chooses to live this far away
Colors muting
Lights on in undraped, uncovered windows
People living
Inside, forgetting the clothes out on the line
Horses standing
On the hill, not noticing the distant car lights as I pass on by
Sharp smell
Of freshly cut grass giving punch to the late summer evening
Giving dimension
To the scene I'm in and an extra set of memories to think about
Heading south
Into the lonely empty stretch, more so than this
Wheels turning
Steadily as my mind turns things over, again and again
Headlights passing
On the other side from someone heading to what I'm leaving
Nearly dark
As blues and purples hue-out into shades of night
Still driving
And I will be for a quiet time much too long

July 30, 2016
Portland, Oregon

I put "Down I-5" by case/lang/veirs on repeat and wrote the image
the song evoked.

Downpouring

After a dry spell
Parched the pages
For far too long
This unexpected
Downpouring of
Words falling fast
Into the mind and
Pooling outward
Flooding pages
Is so welcome
Is so wonderful
Is so needed
Thank you
So much

July 30, 2016
Portland, Oregon

The Joyous Sheen

Lately the joyous sheen
Has been wearing off this city
Where I once could find enchantment
I now find condominiums
Where I used to be able to be inspired
And find my inner peace
Has been turned into an encampment
For an aggressive army of homeless
The metropolitan downtown
Has been overrun by tourists
All carrying pink donut boxes
That traffic which used to be a breeze
Is now a snarling time-consuming dragon
The dream of buying a home here
Has been snatched up sight-unseen
By Bay-Area buyers willing to pay
A hundred grand above asking price –
Something we just can't compete with
The cute little details I loved so much
Adorning people's homes
Are being stolen off their porches
And replaced with absolutely nothing
Making me have to look even harder
Just to find something of beauty
If Portland keeps it up
I'm just going to stop looking
And go somewhere else
To find what I need

July 30, 2016
Portland, Oregon

The Answer

The Answer
To Life
The Universe
And Everything
This year
Is the same as me
Meaning:
If I'm going to
Live up to the number
I need to up my game
And make things happen

        July 30, 2016
        Portland, Oregon

42

July

AUGUST

Out Of The Hatred Closet

It's like the hatred is flowing
From a newly released demon
Rising from the depths
Of America's corroded soul
The one we all thought
Had been put down
So many decades ago
But instead had bided its time
And waited for the right
Moment to revive and rise
Out of the hatred closet
The internet commenters
Were joined by those embolden
By the xenophobe's sound bytes
And came forth, not caring
Who found out they were racist
Not caring who they offended
Not caring about anything
Except cheering at empty promises
And phrases designed to incite
The absolute worst within everyone

August 5, 2016
Portland, Oregon

Seriously, where did all of these racist scumbags come from? Did Trump's open hatred of everything make people think, "Huh, I guess it's ok to hate again"? It's sickening.

Overlush

Oversaturated with color
Brimming
Bursting
Blooming
Overlush with life
Demanding attention
Capturing appreciation
Satisfying everyone
Within sight

August 5, 2016
Portland, Oregon

The beauty of nature here and the sheer number of flowering things is both baffling and inspiring.

In The Neon Playground

There is no happiness here
Ramshackle homes
Starked and weather-beaten
By the ovening sun
The downtrodden residents
Nowhere to be seen
Probably at work
Dressed to the nines
For barely above
Minimum wage
Tending to the needs
Of the high rollers
In the neon playground
Created for them in
Concentrated towers
Looming above the blight
Stretching from rim to rim
Of this desert valley

August 22, 2016
Las Vegas, Nevada

Avoidance On The Strip

After the sun goes down
The crowds come out
Making walking on the sidewalk
More of a Frogger-like game
Of avoidance on the strip
Trying not to trip over
The shaking junkies
Sprawled out, oblivious,
Trying to stay away from
The naked women in body paint
And the Speedo-wearing men
And the badly off-brand
Costumed characters
Reaching out to pull you in
For a pricey picture with them,
Trying not to make eye contact
With the flyer hawks who want
Your attention with the sharp
SLAP SLAP hitting the stack
Of their strip club coupons
Before offering them to your face,
Trying to not get plowed over
By the bachelor or bachelorette groups
Staggering dead drunk down the sidewalk
Four abreast and completely unaware
Swinging their yard of margarita
Like some sort of life-sustaining baton,
Trying to side-step the panhandlers
While trying to walk around and past
The groups of tourists, gawking at it all

August 24, 2016
Las Vegas, Nevada

Leg Of A Rainbow

Leg of a rainbow
Stuck in a cloud
Glowing five times brighter
Now that the rest of the bow
Has dissipated and disappeared
Uncertain as to its continued survival
But there it was, brightly doing its thing
Above the abandoned Walmart
I watched it for a minute or two
Until the cloud moved on
And the rainbow leg went away

August 31, 2016
Vancouver, Washington

August

SEPTEMBER

Sharing The Sunset

A sunset
So bright
So vibrant
That the recently-set sun's light
Shines up from below the horizon
Reflects off clouds above it
Bright orange intensity
Over to the ones on the other side
Pale pink but still lit
Was a wonderful sight
As the Western clouds were caught
In their beautifully selfless act of
Sharing the sunset with the Eastern clouds

September 3, 2016
Portland, Oregon

The Ocean Above

Feet firmly on Earth
Weight and gravity
Keeping me down
But my attention
Is one with the night
My eyes upturned
And searching the sky
Since that's where
My stellar desires lie
Feeling like I understand
Feeling like I'm connected
With everything's everything
The churning galaxies
The flowing energy
The endless expanse
Of the Universe out there,
The ocean above,
Which my earthbound self
Will not get a chance to see
Intimately in person,
Which my carbon shell
Will be unable to travel to,
Will be unable to touch
During this diminishing lifetime
Nevertheless I am connected
On an infinitely deeper level
To all that swirls above
Than feeling any association
Or kinship with the insubstantial
Societal shallow skimming
Which comprises modern life
But like most attention spans
Time is limited and brief
And before I know it
I will be released and free
And finally able to take a dip
In that nocturnal body of water

From the correct vantage point
And explore for an endless night

September 18, 2016
Portland, Oregon

It's been much too long. Too long since writing. Too long since focusing on spirituality. Too long since I last thought about the BIG QUESTIONS of life. This is the person who I am, not the one caught up in spending endless hours reading unimportant news stories or watching shows on Netflix. I need to spend more time like this. It just feels right.

I listened to three songs on repeat while writing this:
Saybia – Bend The Rules
Idlewild – In Remote Part/Scottish Fiction
Lambchop – Sharing A Gibson With Martin Luther King Jr. (live)
I don't know if that's what inspired or focused me, but either way, I'm thankful.

September

The Ocean Above

OCTOBER

The Speed Of Things

The prevailing need
Is the overwhelming thought
The constant increasing of
The speed of things
Always more than before
As a way to cram more
Always more
Into our lives
As a way to match
Our inability to focus
On anything for more
Than a brief moment
So we can experience it
And get on with our lives

October 8, 2016
Portland, Oregon

Do not confuse this with "improvement."

Gorge Gone

Driving home from work
Through the dimmed daylight
Lensed through the uniform gray
Over the big bridge connecting the states
I look to my left, knowing full well
That I won't see the stratovolcano
Sitting over there, fifty miles away
Snow-capped on a clear summer day
But instead, the river
That usually leads to the mountain
Was filled with fog
That erased the entire gorge gone
The cliffs in the distance,
The gentle bend, the marina,
The rolling hills, the scenic overlooks,
All gone, stolen from view by the weather
Who firmly decided
There would be no view today

October 8, 2016
Portland, Oregon

Not What It Used To Be

Things change
We all know that
Go back to the town
Where you grew up
And little things
Here and there
Will be different
The details you remember
Softened with age
Impact hard with reality
As the cherished places
Seeping with memories
Are gone, replaced
And, of course,
Not as good as it once was
Not what it used to be
It never is
But in some places
The pace of this constant
Moves with a swiftness
That may be difficult
For many to deal with
As they are living there
In the situation where
The city evolves
At such a clip
That you have to run
Just to keep up
A favorite hangout
One week
Is sold and bulldozed
And re-christened as a condo
Some months later
Copy, paste, repeat
Block after block
Street after street
Neighborhood

October

After
Neighborhood
And before you know it
The soul of the city
That you fell in love with
Is cratered, is missing, is gone
The magic, which used to be everywhere
Is fading, is evaporating, is dying
And replaced with
Nothing of note,
Nothing of value,
Nothing worth seeing
And after experiencing this
Over and over
Again and again
Day in and out
To the point where
There's no magic left
The question eventually surfaces,
"Why am I still here?"

October 8, 2016
Portland, Oregon

In ten days we will have lived in Portland for three years. On a daily basis we ask ourselves, "Why are we still here?"

I Didn't Need That Calculator After All

Just now
I found myself
Needing to add up
A whole bunch of numbers
So, without a thought,
I pulled out my phone
Thumbed the *Calculator* app
And got ready to add
But something happened
I didn't need that calculator after all
I was able to do it myself
Which surprised the hell out of me
To the point where I felt the need
To tell you about it
Because in this day and age
When one of us can do something simple
Something on our own without the help
Of some kind of computerized device
It feels like a small victory
So, when you find that you did something
Without asking Google, or using your phone
Please share it with someone else
Because we used to do things
And, maybe we still can

October 8, 2016
Portland, Oregon

I was just adding up how many poems I wrote this year. Nothing big.

Everything Wrong With America

Some marketing genius somewhere
Knew exactly what they were doing
When they opened a Pandora's box
The one labeled with the warning,
Everything wrong with America
And released a veritable biblical demon
Upon us and the rest of the world,
Who has done nothing but lie
And purposely spread falsehoods
Who denies saying recorded things
Who purposely stirs up
The worst kind of element
Who thrives in negativity
Like it's an energy source
Who deals nothing but hatred
As if he's working on commission
As the devil's top used car salesman
Who threatens the very fabric of society
Like it was an easy chore
On a daily to-do list
So willing and readily wanting
To incite the easily-led masses
Into embracing their animosity
Clinging to their racism
And outing themselves
Under the planless guise
Of a red hat's slogan
To make America hate again

October 9, 2016
Portland, Oregon

Walkman Nights

When I hear the music
I'm transported back thirty years
To a twelve-year-old me
Just gone to bed
I strain to listen to make sure
The coast is clear
And parents are downstairs
Watching TV
So I reach under my bed
And grab my cassette player
I put on the headphones
Press the large plastic *play* button
And listen to The Doors first album
As the guitars, drums, and keyboard
Along with Jim's familiar voice
Filled me with the music
Of a previous generation
As every note of every song
Burned themselves into my brain
Through repeated playings
While the red battery light
Comforted me in the darkness
Until the tape ended
And I quietly ejected the cassette
Flipped it over, and played the next side
Over and over again
Burning through batteries
Wearing out cassettes
On those Walkman nights
That meant so much
To my younger self

> October 9, 2016
> Portland, Oregon

October

I also sometimes tried to listen to the radio and ended up catching weird static-filled AM stations in French from Montreal, and other stuff like Coast To Coast AM.

Which Is It?

Left work for a quick lunch
So I popped into a Subway
And while the Sandwich Artist
Was busy arting up my lunch
I noticed the tattoo engraved
Permanently behind his left ear
An all-caps, "FTW"
Which gave me wonder, which is it?
Because there are two meanings
The negative one: "Fuck The World"
And the positive one: "For The Win"
As he pressed the pre-sliced veggies
Into the melted pepper jack cheese
I was busy sizing him up
Trying to determine
Which type of person
Was making my lunch
Sure, he was polite enough
But tattoos generally aren't known
As symbols of positivity
And uplifting expression
So I figured the basis for his decision
Was rooted in negativity
And general rejection
Of everything that's good
Which later, when I was back at work
Made my sandwich a little less enjoyable

October 30, 2016
Portland, Oregon

A Cutter In Fronter

Every day
On the highways
My life is continually
In jeopardy
And I am only here
Due to my incredibly
Defensive driving skills
As those who live here
Are stunningly unaware
Of their surroundings
Or, they just don't care
As they merge, weave,
And drive with no regard
For safety for themselves
Or those in their vicinity
There's a cutter in fronter
Here's a red-light runner
That's an aggressive merger
In your rear-view is a car
Too close to see their lights
Thinking nothing of tailgating
That whooshing was a truck
Speeding way too fast
While it's pounding raining
All of which is just normality
For those who hail from here

October 30, 2016
Portland, Oregon

People in the Portland-Vancouver area drive like shit. At least
twice a week I have to act quickly to avoid someone else driving
erratically.

Early Voting

Early voting
Ballot casting
A few days early
Avoiding the lines
Getting it done
So I can feel like
I can stop paying
Attention to the
Political theater
So I can ignore
The pure hatred
Being spewed
So I can tune out
Everything to do
With this wretchedly
Terrible, heinous
Presidential election

October 30, 2016
Portland, Oregon

We're Not Participating This Year

The spooky night
Where the children run free
Well, not anymore
Kids can't be kids like when we were young
That's no longer allowed
Or else the parents will be locked up
When other pratty parents rat them out
Tonight is the night when the children,
With their parents accompanying them,
Go door-to-door in our neighborhood
Yelling the phrase but only expecting
The latter half, because no one dares
To be like Loki and only trick the kids
No, only candy, and here especially
More and more are demanding treats
That are peanut-free, organic,
And gluten-free…yeah, seriously
In past years we haven't participated
But despite our house not being on the list
Of their pre-approved trick or treat route
And despite the porch light being off
And not a lick of decorations on or up
Undaunted by the lack of signals
Saying this is a place you should go
They still bound up our steps
And bang furiously on the door
Driving our dogs mad with rage
Barking to warn us of the intruders
Daring to disturb the sanctuary of our space
On the hope to further fill their bags
Already bulging with a sugary stockpile
Amid the din of dogs howling
And kids' fists pounding
We try and ignore them
Hoping they will get the hint
And move on to the next house
But they don't. Seconds drag on to minutes

And they seem to gain satisfaction
At driving our dogs bonkers
When we can take it no longer
I whip open the door
And am faced with two elementary schoolers
Standing on the dusty rectangle
Where the welcome mat was placed
Until a few hours ago
When I took it inside, just in case,
Their parents, oblivious,
Standing on the sidewalk
As I need to state the obvious
"We're not participating this year,"
And then add,
"That's why we're not on the list,
And why our porch light is off."
The kids stand there, thinking it's a mistake
Until the parents, glare at me for being a monster
And call their kids down, and off they go
I close the door, and we all settle back down
Until three minutes later
When the stomping of feet up onto the porch
Is followed by more pounding
Sending the dogs flying off the couch
Snarling and barking at the door
As this scenario Groundhog-Days itself
Into a continuous loop of cluelessness
Where they ignore common sense
And I seem like a terrible person
Again and again all night long

October 30, 2016
Portland, Oregon

I'm not sure what night is trick or treat night in our neighborhood
this year, but I am dreading it.

October

NOVEMBER

What Should Have Been

What should have been
An easy sailing to victory
Stalled out and died
At the side of the highway
And the oversized truck
With the too-big wheels
The pissing Calvin sticker
While flying the confederate flag
Roared on by much too close
Clipped off our side mirror
Called us horribly racist things
And peeled on out of there
Leaving the majority of us
Wondering what happened
And the rest of the world
Fearful for what lies ahead

November 9, 2016
Portland, Oregon

All Of A Sudden, Everything Changed

All of a sudden, everything changed
Idiocracy is no longer fiction
And is becoming a terrifying blend
Of the horror and documentary genres
As our way of life, albeit flawed,
Was overrun by the orcs from *Lord Of The Rings*
And in many ways, our societal norms
Were regressed by half a century
But the worst aspects of humanity
Have grown by leaps and bounds
As the racists and hatemongers
Used the results of an election
To declare open season
On anything and everything
Different from themselves
Same sex couples finding notes
Taped to their doors calling them fags,
Women run off the road just because
They dared to have a Hillary bumper sticker,
Mixed race couples verbally assaulted
To their faces while at the grocery store
US citizens who look a little different
From the white, white American ideal
Openly told they should be deported
By the neighbors they've known for years
All of a sudden, everything changed
And the America we all used to know
Was no longer the "United" States
But rather two opposing sides:
The bullies, racists, and misogynists,
And anyone they consider their prey

November 13, 2016
Portland, Oregon

Every example in this poem happened to a person I know. America is no longer a safe place for anyone who dares to think, who dares to love, who appears different, or who happens to be a woman. I've always been told that the definition of "insanity" is doing the same thing over and over again expecting a different result. That need to be changed to, "America: November 10, 2016 onward."

Privilege Pass

With everything going on
I feel terrible for my friends
Who don't know if their marriages
Will be repealed sometime soon,
Who don't know if their citizenship status
Will be revoked and they'll get sent home,
Who don't know if they'll be sexually assaulted
Or harassed just walking down the street,
Who don't know what kind of racial taunts
They should be expecting when they go to work,
All sorts of horrible things I never have to worry about
Which makes me feel even worse
Because of the privilege granted to me
By the sheer coincidence
Of my gender, color,
And country of origin
I resent the privilege pass given to me
Based solely on my appearance
From those who choose to hate
The same ones who would despise me
If they could read my thoughts
Like these thoughts written here
But once again, I am safe
Because bullies do not read poetry

November 13, 2016
Portland, Oregon

Escape The Leftovers

Ditch out on the day after ritual
Say no and escape the leftovers
Give that Tupperwared turkey a pass
And go out to do something new
That doesn't involve spending money
Or the expected Black Friday shopping
Avoid the crowded mindless malls
Steer clear of the packed highways
And head out into the pristine nature
To spend an hour or three thinking
About all the things you're thankful for
Giving time to celebrate the spirit of the day

> November 24, 2016
> Portland, Oregon

I lifted the title of this poem from an Instagram post by @thekicey who was advertising her photography at an art gallery. It really stuck in my head and I needed to do something with it.

Such Trivial Things

Militarized police dressed in gear
Leftover from our last failed war
Bullying, terrorizing, and torturing
Working for the big oil company
Protecting their corporate interests
Not those of their fellow citizens
Meanwhile those still in charge
Are refusing to issue the order
That could stop all of this madness
And those who own the cameras
And lease the public airwaves
Are refusing to cover the issue
Fearing it'll expand the problem
The terrible, horrible problem
Of people deeply worried about
The safety of their land and water
Taken by imminent domain and
Now in the hands of an oil company
Previously proven to not care
About such trivial things
Like someone else's clean water
Or how important that land used to be
Because if it actually went down
And there was an accidental spill
The company could just say,
"No. We made our money,"
Declare bankruptcy, and leave
Leaving those who live there
Stuck with the mess they made
Stuck with nothing, nothing at all

November 24, 2016
Portland, Oregon

The Ocean Above

November

The Ocean Above

DECEMBER

Targeted The Woman

In the checkout line at Target
When I saw a woman pushing a cart
Bypassing the checkout lines and heading for the doors
Toddler riding inside, arms and legs wiggling
As it lay in the cart on top of two colorful boxes
Pushing fast past the woman working security
Who targeted the woman, following her out the door,
Shouting, "Ma'am, I need to see your receipt."
A moment later, the woman turned angry
Stormed back inside, slammed the two toy boxes down
On top of the parked line of available carts,
And tried to leave again but was escorted back inside
By security and a manager who pushed the cart with the child
Toward the unknowable confines of the security office
And the impending visit from the police who will taxi her away

December 18, 2016
Portland, Oregon

This was really sad to witness. A young mother caught stealing
toys for her kid.

December

My Pile Of Accomplishment

An hour of time spent
In advance of the holiday
Composing well-wishing messages
Looking up and writing down
The recipients' address information
Picking the right stamp for the right person
Once it is all done and complete
I marvel at my pile of accomplishment
And how good it feels to be ready to send
All of this Christmas cheer

December 18, 2016
Portland, Oregon

I probably should have added a bit about how many weeks we procrastinated until we finally just got it done.

Just Barely, Just Now

My phone chimed
And a message popped up
Stating it was snowing there and
Wondering if it was snowing here.
I looked out my window
Noted the conditions and
My reply, written amidst
My workday busyness,
Was quickly succinct:
"Just barely, just now."

December 18, 2016
Portland, Oregon

December

Thanks For Finally Asking

A woman in the checkout line at Whole Foods
Was about to put her items on the conveyer belt
When she looked back at the man behind her
Who had just a small handful of items
So she made the offer,
Asking if he wanted to go before her
To which he replied, in a spitefully sarcastic tone,
"Thanks for *finally* asking," before rudely refusing her
Left her feeling wounded, hurt, and confused
By the dick's dickish retort

December 18, 2016
Portland, Oregon

Everyone Out Of The Pool

"Everyone out of the pool,"
Said the poet to the phrases
As the final push to complete
The year had arrived on time
The jumbles were straightened
The fragments were completed
The stragglers were left to die
All in a hurried effort to get it
Complied into a new collection
To be released in the new year

December 18, 2016
Portland, Oregon

December

Some Years

Some years are easy and forgettable
They contain smooth memories
That blend away to good feelings
About that general period of time
Some years are hard and memorable
They contain terrible feelings
That form rough, blistered feelings
That still hurt to touch, years later
2016 fell firmly into the latter
With the deaths of so many
Respectable entertainers
With the deaths of so many
Innocent people around the world
With the death of normalcy
As bullies lied and forced their way to the top
Casting a long uncertain shadow
On what next year could shape up to be
Makes me yearn for the years
Which were easy and forgettable
Because I want to have good feelings again

December 18, 2016
Portland, Oregon

The Ocean Above

December

ACKNOWLEDGEMENTS

I would like to thank the following people for their help and support:

My brother, Todd Nixon who helped edit this collection. Of course I think everything I write is typo-less, but he's the one who finds and corrects those errors. Thank you for making me look slightly more professional.

Kari Chapin, my wife, who is awesome and continues to encourage my writing habit.

My family, Sharon Jandrow, Janis McWayne, Ron Chapin and Robyn Chapin, who have given a lot of help and support while I wrote.

Neko Case, kd lang, and Laura Veirs for their brilliant album, *case/lang/veirs* which I listened to on repeat for the bulk of the year.

Abraham-Hicks and the late Dr. Michael Newton.

Finally, and most importantly, *YOU!* I am still always bowled over with amazement when people set aside hours of their time to spend reading my writings. Seriously, thank you. Your continued support is a huge motivator.

IF YOU ENJOYED THIS COLLECTION

Please consider rating it at Amazon.com. As an independent author, having people review my works is critical in helping to increase my exposure and letting new people discover books like this. Thank you!

BOOKS WRITTEN BY ERIC NIXON

Anything But Dreams: A Poetry Collection
Lost In Thought: A Poetry Collection
Emily Dickinson, Superhero – Vol.1
Trying Not To Blink: 2012 Poetry Collection
The Entire Universe: 2013 Poetry Collection
The Taborist: 2014 Poetry Collection
Cascadia's Fault: 2015 Poetry Collection
The Ocean Above: 2016 Poetry Collection
2492: Attack Of The Ancient Cyborg

ABOUT THE AUTHOR

Eric Nixon is a poet and author who has written seven collections of poetry, several short stories, and a two novels, *2492: Attack Of The Ancient Cyborg* and *Emily Dickinson, Superhero – Vol. 1*. Eric lives with his author wife, Kari Chapin, in Portland, Oregon.

www.ingramcontent.com/pod-product-compliance
Lightning Source LLC
Chambersburg PA
CBHW060806050426
42449CB00008B/1571